OVERVIEW

Overview

An engaged workforce is made up of highly motivated individuals who are committed to using their talents and initiative for the good of the organization. Workforce engagement is an integral part of a workforce that has a positive work environment and a strong work ethic. In this course you'll learn how to recognize, develop, and maintain engagement in your workplace.

A positive work environment is key to any organization's long-term success, no matter how many employees you have. It's the leaders who foster the work atmosphere; they're responsible for conducting things in a way that helps raise people's spirits. In this course, you'll learn how you – as a leader – play a vital role in establishing and maintaining a positive work environment, and keeping negativity at bay.

Organizations put great effort and expense into training, technology, and knowledge management - important components of learning. However, the foundation for organizational learning is a learning

Sorin Dumitrascu

culture. In a prolearning culture, employees support continuous learning, which creates positive change. In this course, you'll learn how an organizational learning culture motivates and energizes employees, improves performance, and promotes a positive reputation within and outside the organization. You'll learn the difference between training and learning, and how to encourage employees to drive their own continued learning.

CHAPTER 1 - Establishing an Engaged Workforce

CHAPTER 1 - Establishing an Engaged Workforce

People Are Key for an Engaged Workforce

People Are Key for an Engaged Workforce

For most people, work is necessary to survive. But the need to work goes well beyond an exchange of labor for money.

Work is part of a person's identity. As soon as children can talk, adults ask, "What do you want to be when you grow up?"

In fact, work is a defining characteristic of how people gauge their value to society, and to themselves. And how they feel about their work is measured by how engaged they are.

An engaged workforce is made up of motivated individuals who are committed to using their talents for the good of the organization.

How can you tell if your employees are engaged in their work? There are some signs...

Creating a Positive Atmosphere

You'll notice open communication at all levels — important for building relationships.

You'll observe employees who feel free to share their concerns, ask questions, and offer ideas.

In fact, communication is one of the most important drivers for creating a highly engaged workforce. When organizations actively communicate expectations, employees better understand expectations for their own performance.

Another sign of an engaged workforce is a high degree of collaboration between people and departments. Collaboration is a natural result of people working toward the same goals and objectives. In a collaborative workplace, employees are clear about the purpose of their roles.

Collaboration means employers make a commitment to employees by showing them respect and trust. In return, employees make a similar investment, putting extra effort into meeting the organization's goals.

In an organization with an engaged workforce, you'll notice mutually supportive relationships at every level. Ideas are shared and employees are encouraged to take initiative without fear of reprisal. Since employees are supported and accepted by management, employees achieve higher levels of innovation and efficiency.

Remember to create a work environment in which communication, collaboration, and support are built into established practices, and you'll see more engagement in your workplace.

Improvements Arising from an Engaged Workforce

Improvements Arising from an Engaged Workforce

What does having an engaged workforce mean to an organization? It doesn't mean everyone will always agree. It doesn't guarantee success. And it doesn't mean employees always make the right choices. But an engaged workforce does have advantages over one that's not engaged.

The true measure of the benefits of an engaged workforce is the financial impact it has on the organization's bottom line – how profitable it is.

Engagement has a significant impact on improving workers' performance because of the effort engaged workers will choose to put into doing a good job.

Higher levels of engagement are connected to reduced absenteeism, greater employee retention, increased productivity, enhanced customer satisfaction, and faster business growth.

Engagement also contributes to an organization's competitive edge. Engaged workers are more likely to talk about their organization as being a good place to work. And since creativity comes with engagement, an engaged workforce is more committed to innovation, contributing valuable creations and ideas. This is particularly important for highly competitive companies, such as those in the knowledge sector – and highly creative companies such as design and software companies.

It's not realistic to expect an organization to avoid all the challenges that affect profitability. But employees in an engaged workforce are better able to adapt to and recover from issues that affect the company. When employees are supported in their work, they're more likely to step up and meet challenges. This makes for a more resilient workforce – better able to cope with business crises and setbacks.

Resilience is the quality that helps people get through difficult situations, especially issues that arise from sudden change.

How a workforce reacts to crises, disruptions, and roadblocks is key to an organization's profitability.

The reason engaged employees are more resilient is because their employers have empowered them to act and adapt to change on their own.

An engaged workforce – one that works harder, with less absenteeism, more creativity and resiliency – might not guarantee success, but it's going to help you get there.

Keeping Staff Turnover Low

Keeping Staff Turnover Low

As the engaged workforce creates a positive work environment that boosts productivity, the organization's reputation improves, which helps to retain talented employees. A sure sign of an engaged workforce is low staff turnover.

Engaged employees care about their jobs and their workplaces. This means that they're less likely to change careers.

There are major costs involved in recruiting, evaluating, and training new employees – not to mention stress! Your organization or department must pay for ads, lose work time to interview applicants and train the new hire – or pay someone to do the hiring. The loss of an experienced employee also means a loss of knowledge.

Creating a Positive Atmosphere

Any new hire will make more mistakes and therefore cost more than the departing employee. Keeping turnover low reduces or eliminates these costs.

Retaining knowledge and talent in your company is valuable. Departing employees take knowledge and experience with them. A low turnover rate means talent is retained, resulting in a competitive advantage. When an employee leaves the company, it's often necessary to pull other workers off their jobs to fill the void or increase the hours of employees to cover the work – or train them how to do it. An increased workload results in stress and reduced workplace morale.

Confusion and uncertainty about who is going to replace a departing employee and how the changes will impact the team has a negative effect. Before the employee has even left, they are likely to be unhappy and complaining, which has a negative effect on the team. Long-term employees provide positivity and stability – which makes for better morale.

Teamwork is affected as employees leave. Organizations with low turnover often have established and productive work relationships. Preserving teamwork can mean streamlined work methods.

High turnover can also cause disruptions in service, resulting in dissatisfied customers and lost knowledge regarding projects. Minimizing disruptions helps to keep customers and employees happy. High turnover is a clear indication of a workforce with low job satisfaction. What might your turnover rates tell you?

Qualities that Demonstrate a Strong Work Ethic

Qualities that Demonstrate a Strong Work Ethic

A strong work ethic – is one of the major differences between an engaged workforce and a disengaged workforce. Work ethic is a set of principles an employee uses in the workplace and is related to an employee's belief in the importance of their job, and their commitment to achieving its goals and objectives.

In an engaged workforce, employees' demonstrate their work ethic by aligning their personal goals with the organization's goals. When operational and personal goals are aligned, people at each business level are focused on the same corporate vision, goals, and outcomes.

When engaged employees accept that working toward organizational goals means they're also fulfilling their own goals, the resulting inner agreement means members of an engaged workforce are willing to contribute well beyond the minimum requirements of their ordinary job responsibilities. They're also much more accountable for the results, and they feel responsible for their own actions.

For example, Sam's company focuses on hiring employees who care about environmental issues. They knew he was heavily involved in environmental causes when they went through the hiring process. The company creates a sense of involvement and ownership for Sam since environmental considerations are an integral part of his organization's business practices. This creates an even stronger work ethic and alliance with company goals for Sam.

Because they feel valued and secure, employees are confident being held accountable for achieving results, and comfortable taking responsibility for their actions, as Sam does regularly!

Organizations that encourage engagement support the actions and activities of employees without compromising goals and performance standards. Managers work with employees to set objectives and guidelines. But employees have the freedom to use their creativity and skills to achieve their goals. Engaging people in the workforce means allowing them to make decisions and take ownership of results; in turn, they will contribute well beyond the minimum requirements.

Key Traits of Engaged Employees

Key Traits of Engaged Employees

How do you know when employees are engaged? A key trait you'll notice is that they are emotionally committed to their company and role. They take company values and mission seriously. They care about the outcome of their work. This emotional commitment is the difference between engagement and motivation.

Another trait is that, engaged employees understand and articulate their role. They possess role clarity – a picture of how their job fits into the corporate structure. They relate to their company's goals, and understand how their work impacts the organization.

Engaged employees also know how to utilize the resources of the organization, and take advantage of training opportunities.

Engaged employees will also have the ability to make effective and efficient use of time. They usually like what

Creating a Positive Atmosphere

they're doing, and realize the value of time. They procrastinate less. Making good use of time doesn't mean overwork. Because engaged employees are clear on their roles, they don't deal with false starts or rework.

Employees who aren't engaged rarely give their full attention to their work. In fact, employees who have similar abilities – but different levels of engagement – may produce very different results on the same task!

Another trait of engaged employees is that they build supportive and productive relationships with customers and coworkers. They recognize the importance of working with colleagues. And because they believe in the organization, they become engagement "ambassadors" when dealing with others.

Lastly, engaged employees are comfortable adjusting to change and innovation. This flexibility is essential to an organization's creativity and resilience. Employees who demonstrate engagement are not only adaptive to change, they also devote energy and effort to driving improvement.

Engaged employees are involved in the overall success of their teams and companies. They trust their managers, and in return, they feel trusted to do their jobs.

Engagement Has its Challenges

Engagement Has its Challenges

Workers who aren't satisfied with their job are not challenged or motivated – thus, they become disengaged.

Since people are challenged and motivated by different types of reward and recognition, how do you motivate your workforce? It helps when you understand common challenges of engaging employees, so when you encounter them you can implement strategies to turn them around.

One challenge of engagement is focusing on employees, demonstrating your engagement with the organization even in times of crisis.

To keep employees engaged, simply support them. Employees need to feel that they're valuable partners in supporting the organization. When employees feel devalued, they cease to care about the organization.

Creating a Positive Atmosphere

Another challenge of engagement is creating and encouraging a culture of engagement – where everyone works toward common goals.

Choosing the right engagement strategies, or matching the right incentives to the right employees, is another challenge. It means understanding that employees have individual needs that allow them to work to the best of their abilities.

Engagement strategies include providing learning opportunities, ensuring recognition and rewards are tied to performance, and making sure employees have the resources they need.

And finally, there's the challenge of aligning employees' individual goals with organizational goals. You can address that by showing employees how their efforts contribute to the success of the organization, and how the success of the organization contributes to their success.

If you want to bring out the best in your employees, meet the challenges of engaging your workforce: focusing on employees, creating a culture of engagement, choosing the right engagement strategies, and aligning organizational goals with individual goals. Even the biggest workplace challenges are improved with an engaged workforce.

Exercise: Establishing an Engaged Workforce

Exercise: Establishing an Engaged Workforce

A successful organization requires, at its foundation, an engaged workforce.

In this exercise, you will demonstrate your knowledge of tactics for creating an engaged workforce by

- specifying characteristics and advantages of an engaged workforce,
- recognizing the benefits of low staff turnover,
- specifying traits of strong work ethic and engaged employees, and
- recognizing challenges of engagement in the workplace.

Question

What are the characteristics of an engaged workforce?

Options:

1. Business leaders communicate expectations and are clear about opportunities for employees

2. People at all levels work together toward the same goals and objectives

3. Employees are able to achieve personal and organizational goals because they're supported and accepted by their employers

4. Employees are always willing to work overtime

5. Valuable employees don't leave their jobs

Answer

Option 1: This option is correct. Open communication at all levels is a characteristic of an engaged workforce.

Option 2: This option is correct. A high degree of collaboration is characteristic of an engaged workforce.

Option 3: This option is correct. In an engaged workforce, employees are able to achieve because there are mutually supportive relationships at and between all levels of the organization.

Option 4: This option is incorrect. Engaged employees are committed to the organization, but they'll become disengaged if they feel exploited.

Option 5: This option is incorrect. You can't guarantee you'll never lose employees, but engaged workforces are more likely to retain top-performing talent.

Question

Why is it beneficial to have engaged employees in your workforce?

Options:

1. They'll be more likely to stick with the organization and to be present

2. You can maximize their productivity and potential contribution toward achieving corporate goals and objectives

3. They'll contribute to the organization's competitiveness

4. It will make your company profitable

5. They'll put the goals of the organization above their own goals

6. They'll be more committed to creating and contributing ideas and better able to face challenges

Answer

Option 1: This option is correct. Employee engagement will lead to workers being more invested in the organization and their work, leading to increased employee retention and reduced absenteeism.

Option 2: This option is correct. You'll be able to maximize the performance and productivity of engaged employees because they consider their interests and the interests of the organization to be aligned.

Option 3: This option is correct. Engaged employees are more likely to talk about their organization as being a good place to work, attracting new talent and contributing to the organization's competitive edge.

Option 4: This option is incorrect. Nothing can guarantee financial success. However, engaged employees are more productive, which contributes to higher profitability.

Option 5: This option is incorrect. Engaged employees consider their own interests and the interests of the organization to be aligned.

Option 6: This option is correct. Creativity comes with engagement, so an engaged workforce is more committed to innovation. Employees in an engaged workforce are also better able to adapt to and recover from issues that affect the company.

Creating a Positive Atmosphere

Question
What are some of the effects of low staff turnover?
Options:
1. Reduced costs to the organization
2. Knowledge and talent is retained
3. Enhanced morale
4. Fewer teams are needed
5. People tend to live closer to the office
6. Teamwork is preserved
7. Disruptions are minimized

Answer

Option 1: This option is correct. It's expensive to recruit, hire, and train new employees, so keeping turnover low limits these costs. Additionally, more customers are retained with low staff turnover.

Option 2: This option is correct. When turnover is low, the knowledge and talent of long-term employees is kept within the company.

Option 3: This option is correct. There is less stress and confusion when there is low staff turnover, which leads to enhanced morale.

Option 4: This option is incorrect. Low staff turnover preserves teamwork as people are more consistently working together, but this does not mean that fewer teams are needed.

Option 5: This option is incorrect. The distance people live from the company is not related to staff turnover.

Option 6: This option is correct. When employees leave an organization, teamwork is affected. Low turnover means fewer disruptions to these established and productive work relationships.

Option 7: This option is correct. High turnover can lead to service disruptions, dissatisfied customers, and lost knowledge. Minimizing disruptions by minimizing turnover helps to keep customers and employees happy.

Question

Which elements demonstrate a strong work ethic?

Options:

1. Employees tend to be more reliable and accountable
2. There is greater workforce productivity
3. There is greater alignment between personal and organizational goals
4. Teams do less talking and more working
5. Employees work every weekend

Answer

Option 1: This option is correct. Those with a strong work ethic are much more accountable for the results of their work, and they are reliable because they feel responsible for their own actions.

Option 2: This option is correct. Employees with a strong work ethic feel allowed to make decisions and take ownership of results. In turn, they will contribute well beyond the minimum requirements.

Option 3: This option is correct. In an engaged workforce, employees demonstrate their work ethic by aligning their personal goals with the organization's goals.

Option 4: This option is incorrect. While there will be more productivity, there is typically more communication at all levels in an engaged team with a strong work ethic.

Option 5: This option is incorrect. Engaged employees realize the value of time. They procrastinate less. Making good use of time doesn't mean overwork. Because engaged employees are clear on their roles, they don't deal as often with false starts or rework.

Question

What are the key traits of engaged employees?

Options:

1. They're emotionally committed and consistently demonstrate high performance

2. They understand their roles and make effective and efficient use of time

3. They are comfortable adjusting to change and innovating new ways of doing things

4. There are no conflicts or disagreements when they work together

5. They have fewer extracurricular pursuits than disengaged employees

6. They build supportive relationships with others

Answer

Option 1: This option is correct. Employees need to feel that they matter, that they're valuable, and that they're partners in supporting the organization.

Option 2: This option is correct. A culture of engagement is one in which everyone associated with the organization is encouraged and empowered to work toward common goals and objectives.

Option 3: This option is correct. Effective engagement can only be achieved by matching the right incentives to the right employees.

Option 4: This option is correct. Employees need to understand how their efforts contribute to the success of the organization, and how the success of the organization contributes to their personal success.

Option 5: This option is incorrect. Engagement isn't about making employees follow directions. It's about setting an example of engagement that they can observe and emulate.

Option 6: This option is incorrect. When employees feel devalued, they stop caring about the values, purpose, and mission of the organization.

CHAPTER 2 - Establishing a Positive Work Environment

How Positive Is Your Workplace?

How Positive Is Your Workplace?

How do you know if a workplace is, in fact, a positive one? Fortunately, there are some signs you can look for...

One characteristic of a positive workplace is employee pride, which manifests itself in a number of ways. Look around – are employees answering phones in a cheerful manner and really engaging with customers? Do you notice employees talking up the organization – about its products, management, and staff on social media, at meetings, and at trade shows or other events?

A benefit of employee pride is loyalty – employees think and speak highly of the business, and they want to stick around.

Another easy-to-spot characteristic is teamwork. You can see this when employees are working on a project but it's also visible in other ways. When teamwork's at play, there's a spirit of cooperation among people in different positions as well as between departments.

Maybe during a lunch break, an employee on the design team helps a colleague working in sales improve a presentation. It might be a senior executive who distributes mail around the office, just as an extra excuse to say hello to the employees. And with special events, there is obvious team spirit – whether visible in T-shirts worn at an organization picnic, or the palpable energy at team meetings. Employees in a positive workplace are also visibly happy employees – they enjoy coming to work, and interact with each other in a positive way.

You'll also notice open communication among employees at all levels. They're more likely to be giving and receiving information in person or real-time chat than by e-mail, texts, or instant messages. With open communication, employees don't hear important business announcements secondhand. And their opinions are sought and valued – by the CEO on down.

Observe managers in your workplace – it's another good way to see whether the atmosphere is positive. One sign is managers who encourage. They're interested in their employees, make eye contact with them when they're nearby, and communicate with them regularly. They also set clear, achievable goals for their employees, which helps employees succeed.

And finally, you'll notice that in a workplace with a good vibe, the employees feel valued and recognized for their individual talents. There's often a clear emphasis on individual career growth and personal development. This helps employees to fulfill their own potential – it's easy to see how that makes for a positive workforce!

Once you know what signs to look for, you can assess the level of positivity in your workplace. If you don't see enough of it, then it's time to take action.

Managing Employees in a Positive Way

Managing Employees in a Positive Way

As a manager, your behavior and style are what sets the tone for your team. There a few communication and work techniques that can really help you make that tone a positive one.

One technique may seem obvious, but is often overlooked: giving the right job to the right person. To do this, you must first find out what your employees like to do, what they're skilled in, and where their talents lie. You'll get this information through discussion, direct questions, or simply observing them. For example, if you have a particularly creative employee who likes to decorate the whiteboard, enjoys painting in her spare time, and has past jobs in the art field, you might get her involved in redesigning the organization brochure or web site. On the other hand, you wouldn't assign a particularly shy person who is uncomfortable with public speaking the task of presenting your new product to a large audience. Try to ensure the assigned work is challenging to the individual, as well as interesting.

You also want to set clear expectations when trying to create a positive environment. Ensure everyone on your team knows what's expected of them. So that means clearly state how you expect them to interact with customers and with each other. Clarify how you'd like reports to be presented, and appropriate language to use in e-mails. If an employee doesn't live up to these expectations – maybe by being rude to a colleague or a customer – point it out as soon as possible.

Be sure all employees know their responsibilities, as well as short and long-term goals. It helps if you offer examples and checklists.

Don't set expectations too high, and ensure you set a good example! Above all – be consistent – don't keep changing your expectations or your employees will become confused.

Here's a technique to act on right away – be the manager who provides support to employees to help them succeed. Make sure they have the tools and resources they need to do their jobs well and give them access to appropriate training and equipment. If you ask an employee to use a complicated new software program to create a report, make sure that person receives training first. And provide support by offering guidance, advice, and encouragement to your team regularly.

Don't forget to recognize and reward your employees' hard work, and let others know too, so your team members feel respected and valued. If a team member works late all week to meet a deadline, tell the person how much you appreciate the effort. Be specific about the quality or skill displayed and bring the individual's effort and success to the attention of the team.

At all times, communicate openly and show respect for your employees.

By employing these management techniques, you are well on your way to creating a positive work environment.

Interaction That Fosters a Positive Work Environment

Interaction That Fosters a Positive Work Environment

Leaders typically interact with their employees on a personal level, as well as a professional one – but using some key techniques while doing so can help to foster a positive work environment.

Remember to allow for fun! A fun atmosphere is a positive one. Celebrate events like birthdays, project milestones, awards won by a member of your team, team successes, or employment anniversaries. You could organize luncheons where everyone brings in their specialty and then invite colleagues from other departments to join in – this can promote not only team interaction, but business-wide interaction. Create an environment that celebrates individuality and differences. People are usually proud of their differences – in personality, interests, background, skills, and life

Creating a Positive Atmosphere

experiences – and they bring those unique qualities to the office. In a positive workplace, managers can use these differences to benefit the business.

Notice and accept different preferences, personalities, and work styles, then match these to the most suitable tasks, roles and teams.

For example, individuals who like to work with facts and figures are typically more analytical, reflective, and thorough – so you should place them in roles where these qualities are an asset. Also, a team of mixed work styles is more effective than a team of similar styles. An effective team can comprise employees with analytical work styles and employees with a more creative side. Each employee's strengths support the others' weaknesses – and they will feel valued and supported, rather than redundant.

Encourage each team member to get to know each other, and help to foster a feeling of unity. For example, find out a bit about each employee, and what they like to do outside of work – their hobbies and passions. You can engage them in conversation about these topics at suitable times or arrange team events that involve similar interests outside of work hours.

Make sure, too, that you recognize and reward employees' helpful behavior. For instance, if an employee stays late to help colleagues in another department send out a last-minute order, send a personal e-mail the next day to thank that employee. If an employee volunteers to work over the weekend to create a presentation you need to have ready for first thing Monday morning, thank the individual personally at the team meeting on Monday afternoon.

Sorin Dumitrascu

Acknowledging employee differences and using these techniques to interact with your employees on a personal level, while keeping a professional demeanor, will help you foster a positive work environment.

Beware the Negative Work Environment

Beware the Negative Work Environment

The Business Impact of a Negative Work Environment

As a manager, your responsibilities go beyond that of work production. The emotions and attitudes of your team are also, to an extent, your responsibility. In order to maintain a positive atmosphere, you'll need to keep an eye out for signs of a negative work environment before they take hold.

If you have stress in your workplace, you are likely to have negativity. Nothing breeds a negative vibe quicker than people who are stressed for any reason, but in particular, when there are big changes going on within the organization. Change means instability, and that leads to insecurity – whether justified or not.

Stress can also be the result of a positively changing work environment – for instance, a new state-of- the-art business-wide computer system that no one knows how to use – yet. If people feel they can't handle their job effectively and are moved out of their usual routines, they can lose confidence and become negative.

Reorganizations, mergers, and downsizing can also cause stress as workers can feel a loss of control. Often time getting used to the new situation is all that's needed to overcome these stresses. But if you notice employees becoming argumentative or frequently calling in sick, you must address the issue by talking to the employee, encouraging them, or boosting esteem in the individual or team.

If morale seems low, that's usually an indicator of a negative workplace. Employees with low morale can usually be spotted by their facial expressions, diminishing performance, or frequent negative comments. When motivation is low in the workplace, it points to there being a negative environment. Employees who don't feel valued or challenged are not motivated, and are likely less productive.

In negative work environments, you'll notice that the manager is usually unfriendly and critical. The manager may avoid having friendly interactions with employees during meetings or breaks, for example, and might not even know their employees' names!

Another aspect of managers in negative work environments is that they do not show interest, or give feedback or supervision to their employees. In this atmosphere, employees may be criticized on a regular basis, but they don't ever learn how they can improve their performance. This leaves the employee feeling unappreciated and useless, which certainly doesn't encourage positivity. With a disinterested manager, it's hard for the employees to get ahead or – at times – even know what they should be doing.

As a manager, you should take steps to eliminate any of the signs of negativity from your workplace as soon as they start to appear. Take stock of your own behavior or that of your lower-level managers and make a point of turning your own behavior around for the sake of the workplace.

Behaviors that Improve a Negative Workplace

Behaviors that Improve a Negative Workplace

If you find you're managing a negative work environment, don't despair – you can improve it. And if your workplace is already positive, you play a key role in maintaining that environment.

Certainly as a manager, you face challenges and stresses, but do everything you can to avoid becoming negative yourself. This means not making negative comments about the organization you work for, the work environment, work product, or coworkers. Such comments could make your employees feel uncomfortable and lead to feelings of dissatisfaction – even if employees hadn't noticed the negative situation before. Negative feelings can spread quickly.

For example, don't criticize decisions of senior management – pitting the employees against upper management. There's little the employee can do about such decisions, and negative comments about management are likely to make them feel bitter about the organization overall.

It's also important not to let negativity spread. If one of your employees is always making negative comments, or complaining about the work, other employees, and the organization as a whole, it's crucial to curtail these behaviors. Talk to the employee or employees and take whatever steps necessary to understand and resolve the problem. Often, it's something as simple as an employee feeling they are not important to the team, or not knowing that their work is valued.

For example, if an employee complains that the work and organization are boring and says "there's nothing to learn here," you could offer the person more challenging work. If it turns out an employee's negativity comes from feeling overburdened with work they don't understand or can't handle, you could suggest they enroll in an appropriate training course. And if an employee continues to be negative after you've adequately addressed their issues, it might be time to consider an official warning, or try to find out if there are personal issues involved causing the employee unusual stress.

If you notice there is a widespread negativity issue, you should recruit upper management to help with improving positivity.

You must also make sure you always project a positive attitude and demeanor yourself! Managing with positivity and displaying a can-do attitude toward your job, your team, and the workplace can be infectious. Be cheerful and friendly and focus on solutions, not problems. Look for ways to help your employees succeed. You could translate organization policies into short, easy-to-read checklists and remind employees to follow them.

Offer encouragement and assistance regularly and reward and celebrate the hard work of your team – this helps to increase employee satisfaction and keep your organization a positive place to work!

Exercise: Create and Maintain a Positive Workplace

Exercise: Create and Maintain a Positive Workplace

An organization's long-term success hinges in part on high workplace morale. A key part of your role as manager is encouraging a positive environment.

In this exercise, you will demonstrate your understanding of positive workplace tactics by

- identifying the benefits and characteristics of a positive workplace,
- recognizing management techniques that encourage a positive work environment, and
- identifying the signs and concerns of a negative workplace and managerial practices for turning around a negative environment.

Question

Which examples are signs that you've created a positive work environment?

Creating a Positive Atmosphere

Options:

1. You encourage your employees to follow their career paths, and help them fulfill their potential
2. You tell your employees what their goals are for the next three months, and then help them reach those goals
3. You overhear members of your team speaking happily and excitedly about the company at a social gathering
4. You notice a member of your team helping a junior colleague complete a report
5. Your team works quietly and feels no need to speak during the work day
6. Your office does not give out awards or recognize individuals' achievements

Answer

Option 1: This option is correct. Employees who are encouraged by management and who feel valued usually feel their talents are recognized, and are happy at work.

Option 2: This option is correct. By setting clear goals for employees, and helping them attain them, you display an encouraging attitude.

Option 3: This option is correct. Happy employees who speak positively about the company's activities indicate that employee pride and loyalty are high, which is a sign of a positive work environment.

Option 4: This option is correct. Helping a junior colleague shows that a spirit of cooperation and teamwork exists.

Option 5: This option is incorrect. There is typically open communication among employees in a positive workplace.

Option 6: This option is incorrect. In a positive environment, employees feel valued and recognized for their talents.

Question

What are some ways of creating a positive atmosphere at work?

Options:

1. Organizing a party in the break room to celebrate a team member's birthday

2. Insisting that everyone adopts your style of working

3. Allowing a person to approach a problem from an unusual angle

4. Making an effort to speak with a recently hired employee and asking about hobbies

5. Avoiding any mention of a person's life outside work

6. Sending an e-mail to personally thank a team member who helped you retrieve data after your computer crashed

Answer

Option 1: This option is correct. Organizing a small party for a team member is a wonderful way of creating a positive, fun atmosphere in your office.

Option 2: This option is incorrect. By insisting that everyone adopts the same work style as you, you're not celebrating – or harnessing – the differences that exist between your employees.

Option 3: This option is correct. By allowing people to approach problems from different or unusual angles, you're celebrating the different work styles of your team.

Option 4: This option is correct. By getting to know your team members and promoting personal interactions among them, you're creating a feeling of unity.

Creating a Positive Atmosphere

Option 5: This option is incorrect. You should get to know your team members, both professionally and personally. It's good to know a little about each employee's life outside work.

Option 6: This option is correct. Sending a personal e-mail to thank employees who have been particularly helpful shows that you recognize their good behavior and want to reward it.

Question

What are some signs of a negative work environment?

Options:

1. A manager is highly critical of an employee because of a small grammatical error at the end of an otherwise well-written report

2. An employee looks stressed and unhappy at work every day and isn't performing to the best of her ability

3. A manager is not interested in hearing project updates, and works from home all week without telling his employees

4. A manager considers a suggestion about how the department could be reorganized, but doesn't implement it

5. One of the hardest working members of a team forgets the time and arrives late for an important meeting

Answer

Option 1: This option is correct. An overly critical manager is a sign of a negative work environment.

Option 2: This option is correct. Having an employee with high stress, low morale, and little motivation on your team is a sign of a negative work environment.

Option 3: This option is correct. When a manager isn't showing interest or supervising his employees adequately, a negative atmosphere can develop at work.

Option 4: This option is incorrect. The manager may have good reasons for not implementing certain ideas. However, it's important that managers consider any suggestions they receive, and explain why they're not implementing them.

Option 5: This option is incorrect. An employee arriving late for a meeting isn't in itself a sign of a negative workplace. However, if this behavior is repeated on a regular basis, it could be a sign of negativity.

Question

What are some impacts of a negative work environment?

Options:

1. The team is less creative and less productive

2. The quality of the team's work decreases and their customer service degrades

3. The quality of the work produced by the team has been maintained

4. There is an decrease in employee turnover in the department

5. High-performing employees leave the organization for jobs with lower status

Answer

Option 1: This option is correct. A negative work environment can lead to a decrease in employee creativity and productivity, which can lead to a decrease in product quality and a financial loss.

Option 2: This option is correct. A negative work environment can lead to a decrease in the quality of employees' work and a lack of commitment and loyalty to the company.

Option 3: This option is incorrect. When the quality of work is maintained, it is not an impact of a negative work environment.

Option 4: This option is incorrect. Less employee turnover is usually a sign of a positive environment.

Option 5: This option is correct. When a work environment is negative, employees are more likely to look for alternate employment, even if it means a reduction in salary or status, so they can escape the negativity.

Question

John is the manager of a small advertising agency.

He notices that one of his employees, Candy, acts bored and unenthusiastic at meetings. She calls in sick regularly and, when she does come to work, she arrives late. The quality of her work has also deteriorated.

What should John do to maintain a positive work environment?

Options:

1. Make positive comments about the agency and its employees to Candy

2. Ask Candy to meet with him, so he can find out why her attitude is negative

3. Help Candy succeed in her role by giving her up-to-date guidelines to follow 4. Ignore Candy and focus on his other employees

5. Give Candy a project where she has little interaction with other colleagues

Answer

Option 1: This option is correct. As a manager, it's important John doesn't become negative himself.

Option 2: This option is correct. John must not let Candy's negativity spread to others. He needs to address the issue immediately.

Option 3: This option is correct. By managing with a positive attitude, John is doing his best to maintain a positive atmosphere.

Option 4: This option is incorrect. By ignoring Candy and her behavior, her negativity might spread to others.

Option 5: This option is incorrect. Isolating Candy is likely to make her even more negative.

CHAPTER 3 - How Organizational Learning Drives Positive Change
CHAPTER 3 - How Organizational Learning Drives Positive Change

What Levels of Learning Are in Your Organization?

What Levels of Learning Are in Your Organization?

As a leader, you're already aware that a business relies heavily upon the knowledge of its employees. But learning is not limited to the employee level. There are three distinct levels of learning in organizations: the individual level, the group level, and the organizational level. The three learning levels are dependent upon one another. So learning must be effective at all levels for a business to have a successful learning organizational learning culture. This, in turn, helps to create a positive work environment.

Learning at the individual level occurs when a person acquires a skill, gains knowledge, or achieves a change in attitude or behavior. It can happen through a variety of methods individually or concurrently. Methods include self-study, formal classes, research, or observation. An employee at a bank, for example, might learn the computer system, how to process payments, and customer service etiquette by completing an e-learning course, reading procedures, and observing a colleague.

Learning at the group level is the acquisition of knowledge, skills, and competencies within a group. An orientation session about personality styles would be a method to help bank tellers relate more effectively to each other and to customers. Another example would be if all tellers in a bank were assigned to a group training session in customer service etiquette.

Learning at the organizational level involves the entire learning culture of the organization: the collective intellect and productive capability of its employees. It's achieved through commitment to continuous improvement across the entire organization. Continuous improvement is the ability to improve people's capacity to change and evolve – in other words, "getting better at getting better."

One way to achieve this is if an organization has a culture that is solution focused, which means all employees avoid placing blame during a crisis, and instead learn to actively seek and discuss solutions to issues.

For an organization to be deemed a "learning organization," it must be proactive, not reactive. It must anticipate and prepare for external opportunities and events. The key to success is encouraging and providing opportunities for continuous learning. Ideas, processes, and attitudes must adapt to the needs of customers and the market. This adaptation helps avoid stagnation and creates positive change. Organizational learning influences an organization's culture. A culture of continuous reviews and improvement is more desirable than a defensive culture. A successful learning culture doesn't focus on blame or stoop to using outdated practices.

In order to create a learning culture, an organization's leaders need to ensure that employees at all levels – the individual, group, and organizational levels - have a positive attitude toward learning. It must start at the top and filter down throughout the organization. Everyone must be aware of and enthusiastically accept responsibility for being a learner. There must be a culture of respect, active listening, and effective communication - all of which are vital to drive positive change throughout the organization.

The Difference Between Training and Learning

The Difference Between Training and Learning

Workplace training is an essential ingredient of an organizational learning culture, but a successful learning culture also involves learning. You might think training and learning are synonymous, but there are important differences!

Training is formalized instruction embedded in the workplace focused on teaching specific work-related behaviors or enhancing existing skills. Training is typically structured into formal learning events, like classroom-based workshops or e-learning courses, and participation is usually externally driven by someone other than the learner.

The goal of training is usually focused on improving specific tasks or job-related skills or competencies employees need in their daily job functions, or to meet organizational requirements, such as training employees to use a new computer system, or project management tool. Most of this training is highly structured, formal and planned in terms of objectives, time, or support, and is organized into events such as instructor-led workshops. The purpose is to deliver performance improvement, and the training is intentional.

Training is also externally driven. The need for workplace training is almost always driven by job-related factors, like new hire programs. These programs cover company-specific rules and procedures that employees usually don't need outside of their work environment.

Learning, on the other hand, is the act of acquiring or modifying knowledge, behaviors, skills, or values. The opportunities for learning are ongoing and unlimited – and may occur as part of our everyday lives or our professional lives.

For example, learning negotiation skills as part of a company-provided training program can help a services manager win new contracts on the job, but can also help him get a better price when purchasing a new home. Conversely, a research project an operations manager does on her own time on how to get the best price when buying a new home could help her get a better price on a building she's purchasing for her company.

Learning can occur anytime and anywhere, with or without job requirements or formal training materials. So although training doesn't guarantee learning, it is one of the ways in which learning can occur - but the concept of learning is broader, and allows for accidental learning. It encompasses skills and knowledge most people consider applicable to both work and personal life situations.

Creating a Positive Atmosphere

Learning is a more personal and self-motivated experience than training, and it's up to individual learners to engage in learning opportunities they encounter. It's an active process that requires individual commitment and self-direction to sustain. Ongoing learning is motivated more by personal, internal factors than external factors. When employees are motivated by personal factors, they are engaged and focused on positive change not only within themselves but within the organization.

To be successful, organizations incorporate training that is focused and specific, job related, structured and formal, and externally driven. They accept and encourage learning to be ongoing, unlimited, anytime, anywhere, and self-motivated, and adapt their training programs to optimize the learning process in order to drive positive change.

How to Make Your Knowledge Management Effective

How to Make Your Knowledge Management Effective

Word about "knowledge management" is spreading – so much so that many organizations now have an entire department devoted to it! Knowledge management supports an organization's learning by helping maintain and accelerate access to vital information. While it draws from many disciplines - including information management and networking - knowledge management also involves sourcing, developing, and using knowledge important to the organization. Knowledge management is necessary to support efficient learning, but it's not sufficient on its own.

Knowledge management is not just about data or information. Data is raw material, and information is a collection of this raw material – but knowledge is much more. Knowledge is the interpretation of information in a

Creating a Positive Atmosphere

useful way. Successful interpretation of information requires a learner to draw meaning from it, and make connections that are useful and positive to the individual or organization.

So, on a company-wide scale, knowledge management is the productive use of knowledge to maximize benefit to the organization. To have effective knowledge management, you must ensure that information is available and accessible to all employees.

There are several key activities involved in knowledge management.

Knowledge acquisition is sourcing external knowledge and integrating it into the organization's library of knowledge. This includes relationships with customers, suppliers, competitors, and partners who have the potential to yield new knowledge. Organizations may also choose to acquire knowledge from an outside source if it's cheaper than developing it internally – for example, purchasing a list of potential customers from a distribution company.

Knowledge development supports the acquisition of knowledge by generating new skills and ideas within the organization. It involves using the creativity of employees to produce new capabilities, improved processes, and innovative ideas. For example, an online information input system where tech support employees enter tips and knowledge gained on the job provides their coworkers with the latest information that might not be available otherwise.

Knowledge retention is the organization, storage, and maintenance of knowledge. This depends on the efficient use of electronic media - organizations use popular software tools or proprietary online systems to organize and store corporate knowledge. Knowledge retention is particularly important when there's a high turnover of staff because if an organization's knowledge-retention mechanisms are poor, valuable expertise may be lost when employees leave.

Knowledge distribution involves making knowledge available to employees. It must be readily accessible and easy to navigate when employees need it – this is an asset to an organization. Effective knowledge management uses technology to distribute knowledge effectively. For instance, online corporate libraries might include catalogs of e-learning courses that are distributed by a course-assignment system or on an as-needed basis. These positively affect change by increasing the speed and reliability of knowledge access.

To fully reap its benefits to affect positive change, knowledge management must include acquisition, development, retention, and distribution. This supports the success of individuals as well as the entire organization.

Applying Holistic Thinking and Integration

Applying Holistic Thinking and Integration

How does a leader instill a culture of organizational learning? Well, one of the most important concepts to apply is holistic thinking: where employees understand how the parts of the organization interact and operate together.

Holistic thinking – or systems thinking – is the ability to see the "big picture" within an organization. This means all employees understand how their work contributes to the overall strategy and how changes in one area affect the whole organization. This makes them more committed to the organization and to positive change overall.

A holistic perspective enables employees to understand interrelationships in the organization and learn from them. When a problem exists, employees focus on identifying underlying causes, rather than treating symptoms in the short term. In a positive learning culture, employees understand the strategic importance of their actions. They consider the impact of their actions on other areas of the organization – in the present and in the future.

In order for a group of people to have a holistic approach to thinking, there must be a common organizational vision.

For example, a payments administrator at a bank knows that providing reliable, error-free service is part of the company's vision, and if he makes a mistake on a client account, it impacts the organization's reputation. He also has an understanding of how his actions impact his colleagues. If he's late completing his work, he knows this affects his colleagues' ability to meet a deadline. A good vision motivates all employees, giving them focus, regardless of their place in the organization.

Another important aspect of achieving a common organizational goal to create positive change is integrated learning opportunities, which means learning through a variety of mechanisms. Learners may attend formal training, then reinforce and sustain what they learned through job shadowing, discussion, or on-the-job practice.

Integration includes making learning part of the job, so that employees continually encounter opportunities to grow and develop as they carry out their responsibilities, making them more confident and positive in their work.

For learning to become permanent, it needs to be reinforced, applied, and sustained. This can be achieved by providing employees with continuous reinforcing opportunities, so they can apply what they've learned to everyday tasks. These opportunities should be targeted to learners' needs.

For example, a customer service representative is trained on a new help system that was implemented. She uses the new help system to look up answers for her customers, but also goes through regular training on the updates of the system and how to best utilize it.

When you apply holistic thinking and integrated learning into your learning culture, you help your employees understand where they belong in the organization, and they can naturally incorporate learning as part of their job - both important parts of achieving positive change.

Promoting Change and Collaboration

Promoting Change and Collaboration

While a first step for creating positive change is knowing that your organization needs to change – it's an organization's capacity for change that helps it evolve. Successful organizations are never satisfied with the status quo; they crave continuous learning and improvement. Members of a positive learning culture continually challenge current processes and procedures to ensure relevancy. They also challenge assumptions and perceptions.

So an organization with a positive learning culture will challenge employees' "mental models" – these are deep-rooted assumptions that influence an individual's understanding. They influence that person's behavior and interactions with others. When people are unaware of their mental models, they may not realize the effect they have on their colleagues.

Creating a Positive Atmosphere

An organization that promotes learning must confront mental models in employees, so they become aware of their own assumptions – this promotes self-awareness and self-improvement. Leaders can do this by examining people's views – including their own – in open forums such as team meetings. Managers and leaders should view mistakes as learning opportunities and tolerate and encourage experimentation. Continuous improvement is achieved through learning from experience. When employees are aware of their own assumptions and generalizations, they'll be open and willing to accept change and improvement in the organization and embrace the changes through continuous learning. Consider a sales team leader. She realizes that her hardworking team is overly focused on numbers and targets and calls a meeting to discuss her concerns. Through the members' feedback, she realizes that they assumed performance would be judged solely on meeting targets. They feel the leader undervalues interpersonal skills when considering performance. The leader then decides to challenge the team's perception. Through open dialog, the team members realize their assumption was based solely on hearsay. Here, the team's willingness to challenge perceptions required reflection, analysis, critical thinking, and the courage to change.

Another important aspect of a learning culture is a focus on collaboration. Collaboration is the social – or team – component of learning. It's important because positive relationships can enhance learning while negative relationships stifle learning. People learn best by sharing information - this includes reflecting on problems, putting information in context, questioning assumptions, and giving feedback. This shows a climate of openness and trust, and generates creative tension that motivates people to produce new ideas. Collaboration is much easier when employees have good communication skills and respect the opinions of others...meaningful dialog can't exist without everyone really listening to each other.

All employees must collaborate to learn and solve problems. So group learning and decision making should be standard practice. And when you notice collaborative efforts, don't forget to reward the employees involved.

An organization's capacity for change helps set the stage for a positive learning culture and a focus on collaboration will help grow and maintain that culture.

Getting Employees to Commit to Learning

Getting Employees to Commit to Learning

Once your business has established a positive learning culture, it needs a personal commitment to learning from all employees - this drives employees to take charge of their own learning.

In a prolearning culture, managers realize that energy comes from learning and growing, and they provide tailored opportunities and support to employees to match their unique needs. This means employees are then more likely to take an active role in self-development, setting their own improvement goals, and directing their own learning. Personal commitment is evident when employees seek and take advantage of learning opportunities and when they're recognized and rewarded for learning. Organizations with a positive learning culture create an environment that encourages personal development within the scope of organizational goals.

Employees are encouraged to take charge of their learning in a self-directed manner.

Another element of getting personal commitment from employees is that organizational leaders must work with the unique motivations of each employee. They need to acknowledge that employees have individual styles, personal preferences, and motivators when it comes to learning. Tapping into these motivations and preferences can enable leaders to maximize each individual's potential.

Consider the team leader at a software company who achieves personal commitment from his team by making learning a rewarding experience. He listens to the needs of all team members, and accommodates their work preferences as best he can. For example, he knows the lead designer likes to learn with others and enjoys lively in-person brainstorming sessions. The lead coder, on the other hand, likes contributing her ideas and getting others' ideas through a message board. The team leader accommodates the preferences of both the coder and designer whenever possible. As a result, team members feel motivated and have an incentive to develop their own potential.

Leaders need to go beyond simply providing employees with the information, training, and technology needed to do their jobs. An environment where employees are motivated to take charge of their own learning and encouraged by leaders who work with their unique motivators will help individuals to maximize their personal values and goals for growth and development. This creates positivity within the employees themselves and is an essential ingredient in successful organizational

Creating a Positive Atmosphere

learning. This is an environment where continuous development for every employee - as well as for the organization - is supported. When correctly managed, this atmosphere helps to align the values, goals, and practices of employees with the organization's values and goals, nurturing a culture of learning and creating positive change for the entire organization.

Exercise: Create a Positive Learning Atmosphere

Exercise: Create a Positive Learning Atmosphere

To succeed and flourish in a global market, organizations need positive atmospheres. One way to ensure a positive environment is to support a learning culture in the workplace.

In this exercise, you'll demonstrate your understanding of how organizational learning drives positive change by

- identifying the elements of holistic thinking and integrated learning,
- recognizing the importance of knowledge management, and
- identifying the levels of organizational learning and the difference between learning and training.

Question

Which statements reflect the different levels of organizational learning?

Options:

Creating a Positive Atmosphere

1. An employee learning about customer service etiquette by observing a coworker is an example of individual-level learning

2. A team takes a course on how to relate to each other, which is an example of group-level learning

3. A company adopting a company-wide policy to listen effectively is an example of organizational-level learning

4. A business enrolling its team in e-learning courses they can take at home is an example of organizational-level learning

5. A group reflects on what it learns at the end of each day, which is an example of individual-level learning

Answer

Option 1: This option is correct. Learning at the individual level occurs when a person acquires a skill, gains knowledge, or achieves a change in attitude or behavior. It can happen through a variety of methods, individually or concurrently.

Option 2: This option is correct. Learning at the group level is the acquisition of knowledge, skills, and competencies within a group.

Option 3: This option is correct. Learning at the organizational level involves the entire learning culture of the organization: the collective intellect and productive capability of its employees.

Option 4: This option is incorrect. While a business can certainly enroll its team in e-learning courses to take at home, it is not representative of a level of organizational learning.

Option 5: This option is incorrect. While it is good for a group to reflect upon what it has learned, it is not representative of a level of individual learning.

Question

Match the descriptions to the corresponding activity types. Each activity may have more than one match.

Options:

A. Focused and specifically related to job-related competencies

B. Structured to be consistent and efficient

C. Applied and continued without limits on time, place, or context

D. Motivated by personal and internal factors

E. Can occur anytime or anywhere

F. Externally driven based on job-related factors

Targets:

1. Training
2. Learning

Answer

Training is instruction embedded in the workplace that's focused on teaching job-related skills and competencies. It's highly structured in terms of objectives, time, and organization in an effort to deliver consistent and efficient performance improvement. Training is typically externally driven.

Learning is the act of acquiring and using new skills and knowledge anytime, anywhere. Ongoing, lifelong learning relies much more on individual and personal factors for motivation than any job-related or external factors.

Question

Which activities are involved in effective knowledge management and how?

Options:

Creating a Positive Atmosphere

1. Knowledge development involves using employees' creativity to support the acquisition of knowledge and generate new ideas and processes
2. Knowledge retention relies on the efficient use of electronic media to organize, store, and maintain knowledge
3. Knowledge acquisition involves sourcing external knowledge and integrating it into the organization's library of knowledge
4. Knowledge retention is critical when an organization has low staff turnover
5. Knowledge distribution must be done through a tightly controlled system that can only be accessed through a physical office library

Answer

Option 1: This option is correct. Efficient knowledge management starts with knowledge development, supporting the generation of new skills and ideas within the organization.

Option 2: This option is correct. Knowledge retention involves using popular software tools or

proprietary online systems to organize and store corporate knowledge.

Option 3: This option is correct. Knowledge acquisition involves gathering external knowledge from customers, suppliers, competitors, and partners.

Option 4: This option is incorrect. Knowledge retention is most important when an organization has high staff turnover. If the organization does not have effective knowledge- retention mechanisms in place, knowledge may be lost when employees leave the company.

Option 5: This option is incorrect. Effective knowledge management and distribution means that knowledge is readily available, accessible, and easy to navigate for all employees. Technology is the most effective way to distribute knowledge.

Question

Which statements describe aspects of holistic thinking and integrated learning opportunities?

Options:

1. Employees who think holistically understand how their work impacts the whole organization
2. Holistic thinking involves seeing and understanding the company's "big picture"
3. Integrated learning opportunities allow employees to make learning part of their jobs
4. Integration involves learning through varied mechanisms and then reinforcing and sustaining that knowledge
5. Thinking holistically means focusing on one's own job and leaving organizational considerations to the executive
6. Learning opportunities don't need to be specifically targeted to employees

Answer

Option 1: This option is correct. Holistic thinking means employees understand the strategic importance of their actions and how those actions impact other groups in the organization.

Option 2: This option is correct. Holistic thinking, or systems thinking, is about being able to see the big picture of an organization and how each person's work fits into the overall strategy.

Creating a Positive Atmosphere

Option 3: This option is correct. Integration makes learning part of the job so that employees can grow and develop through their professional responsibilities.

Option 4: This option is correct. Integrated learning opportunities allow employees to gather knowledge and then apply it on the job to reinforce and sustain what they've learned.

Option 5: This option is incorrect. Holistic thinking involves thinking about the big picture and how one's actions may impact other groups and the organization as a whole.

Option 6: This option is incorrect. For integrated learning to become permanent, it needs to be targeted to learners' needs and continuously applied and reinforced on the job.

www.ingramcontent.com/pod-product-compliance
Lightning Source LLC
Chambersburg PA
CBHW020707180526
45163CB00008B/2980